Surfing Among the

CYBER SHARKS

Parent's Guide to Protecting Children and Teens from Online Risk

Vincent Schiavone, Bob Kessinger,
John Sancin and Barb Rose

We dedicate this book to all the parents and grandparents who embrace their responsibility to understand and protect their children in cyberspace and we dedicate it to all children and grandchildren who deserve a safe cyberspace in which to explore and grow.

Contents

Preface

Surfing Among the Cyber Sharks is a parent's guide to protecting children and teens from online risk. It's a collaborative effort written by Vincent Schiavone, Bob Kessinger, John Sancin and Barb Rose, all of whom also have extensive computer security software backgrounds, contributed to the book. It is the first time that noted industry experts have come together to address this important topic.

All four authors work for or are associated with CyberPatrol, one of the leading and most respected names in parental controls software. We have observed a serious digital divide between parents and kids. Kids know the Internet inside out but are unaware of its hidden dangers. Parents have a dual problem: Not only do

they not understand the dangers and consequences of certain online activities; they also
don't know the Internet and what their kids are
doing with it. Thus the digital divide.

While writing this book, we had conversations
with a number of kids to get real-life input on
their cyber activity and experiences. One kid—
we'll call him Jason—was particularly open about
his online activity and some of his personal experiences. Jason's real-life stories are shared
throughout the book, offering unique insights
from a kid's point of view. We thank him for sharing his experiences with us.

Rather than focus on a single aspect of online
risk, such as cyber-bullies or sexual predators,
we explore the big picture, touching on just about
every aspect of cyber dangers. Real-life examples emphasize both the problems and the consequences of surfing among the cyber sharks.

These online threats come from a variety of
places and a wide range of people. Whether the
sources are questionable web sites or online
predators, we refer to them as cyber sharks, people who prey on unsuspecting Internet surfers,

particularly kids. Like real sharks, they are ever present in the safest of waters and they have feeding frenzies in shark-infested waters. We explore the dangers in simple terms and offer practical solutions for keeping your kids safe.

Since we are associated with CyberPatrol, we are able to offer FREE online tools that can help you understand Internet surfing habits and minimize the chances of a cyber shark attack. These tools are available at www.cyberpatrol.com/cyber-sharks and are updated regularly. We appreciate the support we have received from CyberPatrol both in the writing of this book and providing ongoing information and tools to help parents make the Internet a safer place for their kids.

Surfing Among the Cyber Sharks holds nothing back. Protecting kids is a sacred obligation and a clear case where ignorance is not bliss. The more you and your kid know about online dangers, the more prepared both of you will be to deal with and minimize the problems.

Remember that technology does not discriminate between right and wrong or good and bad. People do. That's where you as a parent come in.

And this book will help you protect your children from online risk.

CHAPTER 1

Dangerous Waters

Cyber-bullying, sexual predators and sexual content receive lots of attention in the press and we will cover them in depth in this book. There are other dangers on the Internet that may be just as treacherous to your kid. Every kid has different vulnerabilities and there are many kinds of cyber sharks seeking all kinds of kids.

The Internet just may be the greatest accomplishment of our lifetime. With over 150 million web sites ranging from shopping to social networks, there is nothing that you can't find online. One and a half billion people access information on the Internet and easily connect with others from around the world. And for the most part it's good.

The Internet and technology make our lives easier, letting us do more things faster and better. Now, more than ever, it's hard to imagine life without the Internet, email, cell phones, and texting. But there are dangers lurking in the waters.

Just as the Internet and technology have made everyday life easier for people at home and in business, it has also made things easier for those with malicious intentions. Social issues that have existed forever are multiplied and magnified by technology. Dishing out pornography is easier than sending an email. Child predators regularly comb social networking sites looking for our kids, who we think are in the safety of their homes. Anyone can buy diet pills and steroids as easily as they can download iTunes. And bullying has taken itself from the playground to your kid's computer.

The number and kinds of people using the Internet to exploit kids is mind-blowing. Some want the kids' money. Some want the kids. They know things about your children that even you don't know. And when you look at the statistics, the odds are extremely high that your kid has already been exposed to these people.

Surfing Among the Cyber Sharks paints a clear picture of the online dangers and helps you understand your children's vulnerability to those dangers. It also helps you approach your children to discuss the risks and consequences of online activity, and describes technology you can use to provide a safer online environment. Finally, this book outlines the steps you should take if you encounter a problem.

Sharks in the Water

It's all too easy to take a simplistic view of potential dangers on the Internet. It's not just pornography or cyber-bullying that we need to be concerned about. There is a collection of online bad guys, *cyber sharks*, that in one way or another live to exploit kids.

Like sharks in our oceans, cyber sharks prey on their victims for sustenance and survival. Driven by perverted desire or the potential of quick cash, their target is clear—your kid. Some are blatant, posing as new friends and luring kids into compromising or dangerous situations. Others are more subtle, opening the door to suggestive or inappropriate sites by simply asking for the surfer's age.

Imagine a 14 year old kid at the checkout counter of a store with a six pack of beer and a bottle of wine. The guy at the counter asks the kid, "Are you twenty-one?" The kid says, "sure I am". Taking the kids word for it, the counter guy rings up the sale.

This would never happen in the real world because we have laws to protect our kids. But web site owners pushing porn and other inappropriate material are only interested in protecting themselves. So they ask the kid to check a box indicating they are over twenty-one. That's the only age verification required online.

Cyber sharks come in all shapes and sizes

As a parent, you'd never accept bomb-making instructions mailed to your home, or the local library letting a ten-year-old check out the latest Playboy magazine. Yet kids can get these things online in your own home, your kid's bedroom and often in his school. And if you don't believe it, do a Google image search on Suzie, Susie, or just about any female name ending in –ie. It sounds innocent enough. Do not try this, however, if your kid is around or if you are offended by explicit sexual pictures

Cyber sharks come in all shapes and sizes. While the cyber shark that could inflict the most damage on your child would no doubt be an online sexual predator, your kids are more likely to become victimized by cyber-bullies. Ranging from classmates to casual friends, they use the power of the Internet to spread trash and lies about your kid to anyone who will pay attention.

Like real sharks, cyber sharks continually prowl the waters in search of prey. They may show up in what seem to be safe waters. In these cases we need to be aware of what attracts cyber sharks, and make sure our kids practice safe surfing.

Social networks are a case in point. Sites like MySpace and Facebook serve to connect people in an online network where they willingly share information, photos, and personal interests. It just so happens that this is the same information that sexual predators want. With this type of data at their fingertips, imagine the time they save looking for victims.

Familiar Problems

Most of the problems we face online aren't new. Long before there was a dot-com, we had to confront social problems like child predators, pornography, drug sales, bullying and the like. In 1955, for example, a student in Pennsylvania killed an 18-year-old student who lived in the same dorm in revenge for the 18-year-old's incessant bullying. The simple fact is that these problems exist with or without the Internet or any other technology. Adding technology to the mix makes the situation worse, impacting more people, faster, and with more intensity than ever before.

Anywhere, Anytime

One of the long-standing, and still current, cardinal rules for protecting kids from cyber sharks is to make sure your kids access the Internet in a public part of your home. In other words, don't let your kids surf the net in their bedroom with the door closed. The theory is this: If you keep your family PC in the living room or dining room for all to see, your kids won't surf bad places. While this is still a good practice, advancements in technology and the access to it is changing all the rules. It's no longer about the family PC.

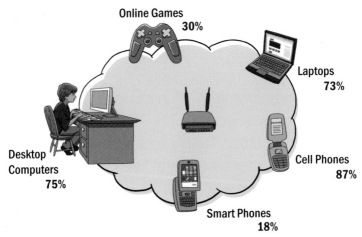

Kids access the Net from anywhere, anytime

The reality is that today kids can go online almost anywhere, anytime. The Internet is accessed not only from the safe confines of the family room but also from school, libraries, work, or a friend's house. And until now, kids have never had more ways to get there, ranging from games to smart phones.

 Seven in ten kids now own or have access to a laptop. And since most laptops have Wi-Fi connections, anyone can go online wherever there is a hot spot, including bookstores, coffee houses, and fast-food chains. Cities and communities are making free Wi-Fi service available to residents. And metrowide hot spots give free Internet access to anyone in the area.

That home Xbox or PlayStation that keeps your kid glued to the couch and TV is now wired.

How Kids Access the Internet

 Three of ten kids are interacting with other gamers online in real time.

 Seven of ten kids have Internet access from a home computer.

 Seven of ten kids have Internet access from a portable laptop computer.

Three of ten kids connect with the Internet using games.

Two of ten kids have smart phones, allowing Internet access from anywhere.

Nine of ten teens have cell phones for texting.

(Source: Lenhart, 2008)

Cell phones have become the universal communicator. Various studies suggest that about half of kids 11 to 12 years old have them, as well as nine out of ten teens. Kids with cell phones text more than they talk, and even use code. And since cell phones almost always have a camera, they are doing something else: "sexting," or sending nude or semi-nude pictures of themselves to others. Two out of ten kids admit to having done this. (Lenhart, 2008)

One in five teens electronically sent, or posted online, nude or semi-nude pictures or videos of themselves. (The National Campaign to Prevent Teen and Unplanned Pregnancy, 2009)

Cell phones also give sex offenders another way to communicate with kids. Like they do in chat rooms, they hide behind the perceived anonymity of text messaging and "talk" to your child.

How the Waters Get Infested: The Technology Multipliers	
Massive	150 million web sites worldwide.
Instantly Accessible	1.5 billion people worldwide with instant access to anything you put online.
Unbiased	Technology doesn't care about content.
Portable	Kids don't need computers at home to get online.
Advanced	Kids know technology and parents can't catch up.
Anonymous	Technology makes it easier to hide activity and identity.
Efficient	Easier and faster for sharks to find kids.

You simply can't be with your children every time they go online. Nor can you hope to keep up with the latest in technology. Most of the stuff we use today didn't exist just five years ago. And since we couldn't imagine back then the technology we have today, we can't imagine today the technology we'll need to deal with in the future.

What to Do?

The first step is to acknowledge the breadth, depth, and seriousness of the problem. Sounds simple, but in practice, most parents have no idea of the kinds of things kids are exposed to online every day. And when something strange or bad does happen, the odds are your kids won't tell you about it.

 Seven out of ten kids do not tell their parents or guardians about what they do online unless asked. (McAfee, 2008, p.3)

The most disheartening and alarming reaction to cyber sharks is that most parents believe the issue is being addressed because they talk to and trust their kids. Trust and communication are good things. Unfortunately, however, even smart, good kids do stupid things. And in many cases, as smart as kids are about technology and the Internet, they don't have enough information about the risks and consequences to make good decisions. And that can be disastrous.

There is also a fear among parents of violating their kid's privacy. But on some level, isn't paying attention to things children may want to keep private part of a parent's job? If we are too afraid to intrude, we miss opportunities to discuss important issues facing our kids.

We would never let our kids run free in a real-world place that had everything the Internet has to offer. We can't afford to do it in the virtual world, either. And although kids may not like it, we must take these steps to ensure that our kids are adequately protected.

The bottom line is that protecting our minor children online is a parent's right and responsibility. This isn't about their freedom to view or freedom of speech. It's simply about keeping our kids safe from ever present dangers for their own good.

Protecting Your Kids

Here is a summary of the steps you can take to protect your kids online:

☐ Understand the Internet and cyber sharks.

☐ Talk to your kids about their online activity, the risks, and the consequences.

☐ Use appropriate technology to help with the problem, such as blocking access to bad sites (shark-infested waters).

☐ Trust but verify. Monitor your kids' online activity.

☐ Watch what's happening in open waters. Know what's happening outside your own virtual world.

☐ Create an emergency response plan in case the cyber sharks attack.

Each of these steps is covered in detail in the chapters that follow.

Meet Jason, Our Undercover Kid

 Jason is a 16-year-old high school student who agreed to talk with us about his personal cyber experiences and give us honest answers to our questions. He's a good kid, has plenty of friends, is socially active and has a great relationship with his parents. In fact, his father was with us as we asked questions and shared stories.

Like many kids his age, Jason knows the Internet. He has a Facebook account, participates in chat rooms and knows exactly where to go on the Internet to find any information he needs. He even showed us a few things we weren't aware of. However, like many other kids we talked to, he had no idea how cyber sharks work or what they do.

Jason doesn't use the Internet to intentionally do bad or malicious things. He's just trying to survive in a cyber world. All of what he knows about the Internet he has learned on his own or from his friends. That includes cyber values. Since his parents don't really understand the Internet, they can't teach him, so many of these values come from his friends. For example, "If they're doing it, it must be OK."

We'll use Jason's experiences throughout this book to help give you a better understanding of what a typical kid is doing online. We thank him for sharing his experiences with us

CHAPTER 2

Playing in the Cloud

Computer people refer to the Internet as *the cloud*. Before dipping your toes in to test the cyber water, it's important to understand a few facts about working and playing "in the cloud."

Some Basic Facts

- First of all, *what happens in cyberspace stays in cyberspace—forever.* The Internet is a two-way street. You can get information or give it. But once you give it, there's no taking it back.

- Next, *there is no such thing as age verification online*. When required, give an age, any age, and you've satisfied the requirement.

- Finally, *anyone can operate with almost complete anonymity*. Almost. So kids who believe they are anonymous need to understand that most online actions are traceable; in many cases there is only the appearance of anonymity. But it's most important to remember that cyber sharks also can appear to be anonymous.

No Delete, No Undo

While a good portion of this book deals with cyber sharks who come after kids, this section is a little different. It's about shark bait. One of the best ways to protect your kids is to be sure they don't put things online that will attract cyber sharks. And what most people, adults as well as kids, don't understand is that when you use the Internet to share information, it's there forever. It becomes shark bait.

Ever send an email that you'd like to take back? It can't be done. OK, so you send another email taking back or apologizing for the first.

Sharing information online, private or public, puts it out to the world. Once you post information to a social networking site, send or reply to an email, text or post a picture, or comment on a blog, it's out there for anyone to see. In some cases it's stored in a database you can't control. In other cases it's passed on from the original recipient to whomever they care to share it with. In either case there is no undo.

Kids willingly and knowingly give up information without considering the consequences. Even if you've taught them that giving out information like home addresses and phone numbers is strictly taboo, social networking sites give them the opportunity to offer up much more without knowing it.

For example, posting seemingly innocent pictures can unwittingly divulge important information. Take a picture of a cheerleader, standing in front of her house, with the address showing. From just this one picture, any interested observer can find just about everything they need to know about her.

Posting inappropriate pictures can have even greater consequences. Drinking at a dorm party and posting the picture may seem cool to your kids now, but a few years down the road, potential employers might not think it's so cool.

Some prospective employers are asking applicants for access to their Facebook or MySpace page as part of the interviewing process. Employers can terminate an employee or refuse to hire a job applicant based on information found on the Internet. High schools are also warning students that college admissions officers surf Facebook.

 A public university denied a woman a teaching degree because of a photo posted on her MySpace page with the caption "drunken pirate." (The Wired Campus, 2008)

And here's the real rub: Information or pictures shared on the Internet are out there somewhere; there's no guarantee you can delete them. Then there are those pictures sent to others or shared on Facebook. You can't retrieve or delete pictures sent to others, and you can't control what others do with pictures posted online.

So to protect your kids, don't let them put things online that will attract cyber sharks. And remember that once those things are "in the cloud," they're not going away. Even if you want to try and remove unflattering data, it can be very expensive, with no guarantees of success.

No Age Verification

You can be any age you want to be online. Kids can pretend they are adults and adults can pretend they are kids. And it's easy. How is that possible? Anyone asking you to verify or confirm your age simply takes your word for it. There's no verification.

The prevailing attitude of sites that ask your age is that they don't really care how old you are. If they state that you must be 21 to enter their site, or if they just ask you to enter your birth date on an application form, they've done their job. The law only requires sites to ask a user's age and they are in the clear, even on kid sites. It may be wrong, but it's the law. And if you wonder why they don't verify, follow the money. The internet is big business and there is lots of money that can be made from kids online.

There are two sides to this age problem. The more obvious problem is that kids can lie about their age to gain access to sites that are adult-oriented or that offer access to age-restricted items like drugs, alcohol, or gambling. Conversely, adults can pretend they're kids and make their way into chat groups and social networking sites. And that's exactly what sexual predators do.

In January 2009 a Supreme Court decision took "online age verification" off the table as a requirement of the Child Online Protection Act (Neuberger, 2009). So when it comes to the Internet, we are pretty much stuck with trusting kids and adults to give their real ages.

 The U.S. Supreme Court refused to resurrect a law requiring web sites containing "material harmful to minors" to restrict access based on age. (Gross, 2009)

Hidden Identity

Whether you're sending an email or filling out a form, it's difficult, if not impossible, to verify that you are who you say you are. If you create a fictitious name and get yourself a free email address that alone will get you past the gates of most restricted web sites requiring you to register. So even if your kids have email addresses you know about, it doesn't mean they don't have others you don't know about.

Kids can set up multiple emails for multiple purposes. Let's say they want to join a site that requires an email address but they want to keep their membership hidden from their parents. Creating a secret email account makes it easy. They don't have to access the email account from the computer's email program (like Outlook); they can access it directly from the provider's web site.

Very little information is required for setting up an email account, and there are plenty of free email services available. Just supply a name (not verified), age (not verified), and password, and you're off to the races. And kids can use any

"handle" they want for their e-mail address like:
mycityhotblonde18@AOL.com

What's needed to get a free email account	Google Gmail	Hotmail (Microsoft) [1]	Yahoo	America Online (AOL)
First and Last Name	✱	✱	✱	✱
Gender	✱	✱	✱	✱
Birth Year	✱	✱	✱	✱
Security Question (and Answer)	✱	✱	✱	✱
Secondary (Alternate) Email Address ✱	✱	✱	✱	✱
Current Geographical Location (Country)	✱	✱	✱	✱
Terms of Service Agreement	✱	✱	✱	✱
Accept/OK button	✱	✱	✱	✱

1=Utilizes Windows Live ID
✱=Optional in Google Gmail registration

Very little information is required to get a free email account

CHAPTER 3

Shapes and Sizes

The two main types of cyber sharks, *attracters* and *attackers*, feed on the easiest prey: kids.

All kinds of cyber sharks lurk in the apparent calm of the Internet waters. Some are out there casting nets to see who they can collect to come to their web sites. Others are looking for information about kids so they can steal identities. The ultimate cyber sharks are sexual predators, and they literally go after kids.

There are two main types of cyber sharks: attracters and attackers. *Attracters* lure kids to objectionable web sites, preying on their youthful curiosity. *Attackers* are outright predators who will do harm using any means possible.

 A Wisconsin high school student was facing felony charges for posing as a girl on Facebook and tricking 31 male class-mates into sending him naked photos of themselves. (Associated Press [AP], 2009)

There are two other, passive participators in the world of cyber sharks: *enablers*, and *smart kids who do dumb things*. Enablers are typically social networking sites that serve the positive purpose of sharing information and connecting people with common backgrounds or interests. Unfortunately, these are all the things that predators are looking for.

Predators need information about their prey, and they also need to connect with them. That's why MySpace, Facebook, and other social networking sites are a virtual gold mine for sexual predators.

 Over the course of two years, MySpace kicked 90,000 known registered sex offenders off its web site. (Schonfeld, 2009)

Attracter Cyber Sharks

Attracter cyber sharks use web sites that kids willingly or mistakenly go to that display undesirable or harmful content. Most often, these websites contain adult content or they are porn sites. But there are plenty of harmful web sites that contain no adult content whatsoever.

Kids are curious and attracters know it. Simple searches produce results that get kids to these web sites. Sometimes they find their way there using a link sent from a friend.

Another trick that attracters use to pull in visitors takes advantage of typos and spelling errors that occur when the user mistypes a web address. It's called *ambush porn*. Nearly four out of ten kids have experienced it. Your kid can make a simple typing mistake and end up in a very bad place.

For example, kids frequently visit YouTube (www.youtube.com). But if they mistakenly add an extra y (www.youytube.com), they are whisked away to a very graphic XXX site.

We strongly suggest that you DO NOT TRY THIS. Once you arrive at youytube.com it takes control of your browsing and you may have a tough time leaving the site.

Many web sites are inappropriate for children and teens. The categories of sites listed here are those that no kid has any business being on. Information on these sites is vulgar, lewd, or out-right illegal.

Adult Sites contain adult topics, phone sex, adult chat rooms. Nudity may be included, but not graphic sexual content. *XXX Sites* contain porno-graphic and graphic adult material.

Gambling Sites offer online gambling, bookmak-ing, sports betting, dog tracks, and horse race betting. *Warez* and *Hacking Sites* discuss or dis-tribute tools for hacking, cracking, attacking, or phreaking systems. They offer software that has been cracked or that has a key generator, which provides a key to open the application you are trying to use for free. Much of this activity is ille-gal.

Drug Sites contain illegal online pharmacies, illegal drugs, drug manufacturing, and information about recreational drug usage. *Illegal Activities Sites* describe how to modify weapons, make bombs, phish, and perform credit card fraud.

Adult and XXX Sites

The difference between adult and XXX sites is the degree and level of unsuitable content on a web site. Adult content may be limited to nudity and suggestive material. XXX sites are all-out pornography.

Four out of ten kids admit to viewing porn, nearly half of whom say they didn't want to see it. So even if your kids have no desire to look at porn, there's still a fairly strong chance that they'll get ambushed by a site that's just waiting for them to make a typing error. Simple, innocent searches can also display links to porn sites.

 The average teen spends 1 hour and 40 minutes a week browsing sites for pornography. (Daily Mail Reporter, 2009)

Popular search sites like Google and Yahoo! offer a safe searching feature (shown below) that removes sexually explicit material from search results. And the good news is that they come pre-set to block porn. But some cyber-savvy kids know this. So they change the settings to allow porn to show up in searches. If they know you are paying attention, they change the setting back when they've finished. They get to the porn and you never know

---

SafeSearch Filtering

Google's SafeSearch blocks web pages containing explicit sexual content from appearing in search results.

○ Use strict filtering (Filter both explicit text and explicit images)
○ Use moderate filtering (Filter explicit images only - default behavior)
◉ Do not filter my search results.

A view of the Google Search SafeFiltering features

To turn on, or change, Google's Safe Search Filtering, go to Preferences and select either the strict or moderate filtering option. The Yahoo! Safe Search Filter can be accessed through the Yahoo! Search preferences.

Most schools and businesses, and some homes, use software to block access to these sites. But cyber-savvy kids have that figured out too. There are web sites and even videos that teach kids how to get to blocked sites through something called proxies. Good parental controls software, like CyberPatrol, blocks the proxies. But what may be even more enlightening here is that some kids are working hard to get to these blocked sites.

Jason on Viewing Porn Sites

 To be honest, we still aren't entirely sure how much time Jason may be spending at porn sites, if any. We asked, "How many times do you go to porn sites?" Jason said, "I don't"—followed by, "You just have to make sure that safe surfing is turned off if you want to view them." He then went on to show us exactly how to do it.

Spending time on porn sites can also cause problems with computers. According to Web of Trust (WOT), "Websites offering adult content are the single most significant security threat for Internet users, comprising 31 percent of dangerous websites." Adult and XXX sites account for the largest percentage of web sites from which viruses are spread. (Web of Trust, 2008)

Gambling Sites

Now that gambling has found its way to TV and Texas Hold 'Em has become increasingly popular, kids are trying their hand at online gambling. Some games are free and for others you pay to play.

While most online games and activities are legal for minors, gambling is not. The law requires a person to be 18 to gamble online. So how do young kids get around the law? By simply clicking a button that says they are 18 years old, and paying with a parents credit card.

VISITED A GAMBLING SITE

The Unlawful Internet Gambling Enforcement Act of 2006 bars online casinos from doing business in America and restricts financial institutions from processing their transactions. Yet Internet casinos are still available and some kids are finding technical workarounds to evade the rules and gamble online.

Two to seven percent of kids have a serious gambling problem. Another 10 to 14 percent are at risk for developing a serious gambling problem. (Aleccia, 2009)

Kids who gamble can lose real money, and even worse, risk becoming addicted to gambling. Two of ten kids have visited gambling sites. The National Center for Responsible Gambling reports that 2 to 7 percent of young people experience a gambling addiction, compared to about 1 percent of adults.

According to Mary Lay, project manager with the Indiana Problem Gambling Awareness Program at Indiana University, "Online poker rooms have made it that much easier to gamble at all hours of the day. College students can always name that one guy or girl always in their room, playing poker." (Brooks, 2009)

Warez and Hacking

Warez (pronounced "wayrz" or "wayrss") is a dubious way of obtaining software that has been cracked or that has key generators that give you illegal keys that open software. The  term is generally used to describe pirated software made available to the public. Crackers break the software's protection and then share illegal copies. They then distribute them via the Internet.

Fourteen college students were sued for copyright infringement by the recording industry's trade association, which accused them of illegally downloading or sharing music files over the Internet. (Swedlund, 2008)

ILLEGALLY DOWN-LOADED MUSIC

Peer-to-peer (P2P) or person-to-person Warez sites allow users to share files (music, video, and so on) with one another. The entertainment industry contends that sharing music and movies online is illegal. As a result, it has filed and won lawsuits against kids sharing files illegally. According to industry sources, three in ten kids have illegally downloaded music.

Jason on Illegal Downloading of Music

We asked Jason if he had ever downloaded music illegally. "Sometimes," he said. "Everybody does it. But if I really like the artist, I delete the file and go out and buy the actual CD."

He went on to say that some lesser-known artists post their entire albums for free. It was his way of saying that some of what he is downloading is legal.

We then asked Jason if he had downloaded anything else. "Just movies and stuff," he said. "You can get newer movies before anyone else. They're just out there."

None of this sat very well with Jason's dad. He had already told Jason to stop, but obviously Jason hadn't. Yet these types of sites are easily blocked with parental controls software.

We told Jason about the consequences this way: "You are putting your mom and dad, your way of life, your college education, and your parent's reputation on the line. Is it worth all that to simply get a free song you like?"

He was a bit stunned and said, "Wow, never thought about it that way. Don't think I want that to happen."

"So are you going to stop?" we asked.

"I'll have to really think about that the next time I download music," he said.

The problem extends beyond music. Kids also download bootlegged movies and other videos. And from what we've been told, they don't see what the real problem is here. Make no mistake about it, this is illegal and could cost you, the parent, big bucks.

This problem is easy to solve. You can use filtering or parental controls software to block these download sites and give your kids the time they need to understand the potential legal consequences of illegally downloading music and videos.

There are Warez sites that can be trusted and that offer legitimate free music, games and more. Still, using these sites is a risky thing to do, because they could be exposing your computer to viruses, spyware, and other unwanted software.

 Parents and guardians can be held responsible for what happens on the family computers even if they are not themselves engaged in illegal activity. (Childnet.com, 2008)

Buying Drugs Online

 A Columbia University study found that eight out of ten web sites selling potent prescription drugs (OxyContin, Valium, and Ritalin) did not ask for proper prescriptions. Of that group, nearly half specifically said that no prescription was needed.

Think of the implications. You don't need a prescription and there is no real age verification to purchase potentially lethal and addictive prescription medication. With a credit card, kids can buy drugs online as easily as they can download music.

The Partnership for a Drug-Free America says that nearly two in ten teens report abusing prescription medications to get high, and one in ten report abusing cough medicine to get high (The Partnership for a Drug Free America, p. 17, 2009). The Internet makes it easy for kids to get these drugs.

ABUSED Rx DRUGS

A 2007 report by the U.S. Drug Enforcement Administration (DEA) estimated that only 11 percent of prescriptions filled by traditional pharmacies were for controlled substances, compared to 80 percent filled by Internet pharmacies. This is an amazing reversal and points to the availability and relative ease of obtaining controlled substances over the Internet.

Illegal Activities

The illegal activities category covers a wide range of sites, with topics that include modifying weapons, bomb-making, phishing, and credit card fraud. In some ways these sites represent the darkest and most irresponsible side of the Internet. Why would someone need to learn how to build a bomb? Good question! Yet not only are written directions available for making bombs, but you can find instructional videos on YouTube, as well.

In Japan a 16-year-old boy was arrested on suspicion of trying to manufacture a bomb to blow up his classmates. He had gotten tips from the Internet on how to make bombs. (Foxnews.com, 2009)

Other YouTube videos show you how to hack credit cards. And there's similar information about credit cards that could easily tempt kids to try other things they wouldn't normally consider.

Private Collections

Each kid has their own private collection of favorite web sites that varies as widely as kids themselves. Some sites are good, others are inappropriate, and some are outright dangerous and filled with cyber sharks just waiting to lure kids into their trap. Sites can come from friends or from just searching on the Net.

Jason on Viewing Inappropriate Images

 One of Jason's favorite web sites is 4chan.org, which bills itself as a simple image-based bulletin board where anyone can post comments and share images. He goes there because he's interested in animé (pronounced "ann-uh-may"). Animé is a style of Japanese comics that is very popular in Japan and is gaining popularity in the U.S. and around the world. Jason goes there to look for and post animé drawings.

Here's the rub. As billed in the web site's description, anyone can post anything here, including "Sexy Beautiful Women," hard core, and more. You just need to say you are 18 and accept, among others, this term: "By clicking 'I Agree' and then viewing our site, you agree not to hold the webmaster and staff of this site liable for any damages from your use of these boards."

Of course, Jason never read this agreement until we pointed it out to him. And does he wander away from animé into the darker side of this site sometimes? Yes, he does.

Attacker Cyber Sharks

The most dangerous type of cyber shark is the attacker. As opposed to luring kids to inappropriate web sites, these predatory cyber sharks aggressively pursue kids for the purpose of causing harm. They know the Internet and how to exploit kids who use it.

There are three main kinds of attacker cyber sharks:

- *Cyber bullies* create threatening messages or spread rumors about others online. Their motivation can be anger, revenge, or frustration.

- *Identity thieves* steal identities for an illegal purpose such as accessing bank accounts or credit cards. Identity thieves are usually after money.

- *Sexual predators* pursue kids for the purpose of sex.

All three attackers can be life-damaging. Cyber bullies and online sexual predators can cause death to their victims. Constant cyber-bullying has resulted in suicides. Cyber predators are unpredictable, and the results of their activities range from molestation to murder.

 Search for the term *bullycide* on YouTube, Google and other search engines to learn more.

Cyber Bullies

Cyber bullies are the modern, techno-logically advanced versions of the old-fashioned schoolyard bully. They have all the same social characteristics and the same motivation, but they have much better tools to intimidate, harass, and torment their victims.

Four out of ten kids have been bullied online, and five out of ten admit having typed mean or hateful things about class-mates themselves.

A great deal of attention is being paid to cyber-bullying, due mainly to its potentially dire conse-quences. Bullycide, or suicide prompted by bully-ing, is the ultimate bad result. Kids are taking their own lives because they can no longer take the constant bullying. Unfortunately, blocking a web site or controlling computer use won't stop this problem.

 The Australian Clearinghouse for Youth Studies says that a main reason that kids who have been harassed online don't report it is the fear of losing their access to technology. (Maher 2008, p. 50-57).

Cyber bullies use both the Internet and cell phones to threaten others, spread rumors, and even post images. And since images can be easily altered using Photoshop or other image editing software, cyber-bullying takes on a whole new dimension. It's quick and simple, and it can reach millions of people.

Jason on Cyberbullying

 Jason was an early victim of cyber-bullying. It started in middle school when he and a friend pranked a kid named Damian. According to Jason, "My friend blamed me for the prank, so Damian came after me. Somehow he guessed or cracked my passwords to my instant-messaging sites. Then he logged in as me and started saying a bunch of bad things about and to my friends. They all hated me."

Things got so bad for Jason that he wanted to transfer to another school. And he never told his parents or a teacher. He lived through it and dealt with it on his own.

Remember that Jason has great parents and he's a good kid. But most kids won't talk about these types of experiences unless parents ask. When we talked further about it, neither Jason nor his parents knew the right steps to take.

In some cases kids fall victim when their password or other personal information is stolen. Using that information, the cyber bully sends false messages from the victim's email address, posts them on their personal web site, or adds them to their social networking site.

Cyber bullying has become an epidemic. The shield of perceived anonymity provided by the Internet emboldens some kids to prey on others. It also lets "good kids," who themselves have been bullied, strike back. And because many kids are smart and technically savvy, they know how to create many aliases that allow them to say or post whatever they want in chat rooms and social networking sites without identifying themselves.

The increase in cyber-bullying has caused schools, law enforcement, and government regulators to be concerned and take action. The increase in child and teen suicides directly related to cyber-bullying has social scientists and educators frightened, and with good reason.

Kid Identity Thieves

One would think that kids, especially younger ones, have little to offer identity thieves. So why check whether a credit report has been issued under a child's name? According to Debix, a company specializing in identity protection, the unlikelihood that a parent would check is exactly what makes children easy targets for identity thieves.

Debix reports that among the five percent of kids who have credit reports, there was an average of $12,779 in fraudulent or wrongly assigned debt.

KID VICTIMS OF IDENTITY THEFT

The Internet is a great place for identity thieves to go after information from kids, especially from younger kids. They are innocent and naive. Cyber sharks in chat rooms or on social networking sites know just what to say to get a kid's confidence. They can even offer "cyber candy," like cyber club points, to get the information they want.

 According to the Debix study, 5 of every 100 kids have credit reports under their Social Security number. Three of every 100 were victims of identity theft. (Vamosi, 2008)

Sexual Predators

Sexual predators are the most dangerous kind of cyber shark, and all our children are at risk. The ultimate goal of sexual predators is to meet kids in the real world and have sexual contact with them. Because the Internet puts personal information, communication tools, and kids at their fingertips, it creates the "perfect storm."

According to Pew/Internet, three out of ten online teens have been contacted by a complete stranger. Nearly one in ten experienced disturbing stranger contact. The same survey reports that social network users are more likely to be contacted by strangers.

The National Center for Missing and Exploited Children reports that one in seven kids online has been solicited or enticed. (National Center for Missing and Exploited Children, p. 15, 2009)

There is a good chance that if your kid is contacted by an online stranger, you won't know about it. When confronted with the situation, only 3 in 100 kids told an adult or someone in authority.

CONTACTED BY A STRANGER

Online sexual predators are experts in using the Internet to lure kids into real-world meetings. They are on social networking sites, they're in chat groups, and they use instant messaging and even cell phone texting to stalk their prey. According to *Enhancing Child Safety & Online Technologies*, those who harass online don't bother to hide their ages or intentions. They are up front with potential victims. "In the majority of cases referred to law enforcement, adult offenders are honest about being an adult, and in 79 percent of the cases, they are honest about their intentions to have sex with the youth." (Palfrey et al. 1994, p. 262)

Enabler Cyber Sharks

Enabler cyber sharks are legitimate Internet web sites that offer services that can be easily used to conduct questionable or illegal activities, specifically with kids. On the surface, these sites and services appear totally harmless. Criminals and cyber bullies find clever ways to use them to their advantage. It's easy to mistake cyber sharks for dolphins. The most prominent enablers are social networking sites and chat rooms, followed by virtual worlds, instant messaging, and video-sharing sites.

Social Networking Sites

Social networking sites (SNS) are web-based services that allow users to create a public profile and share it with other users within the network. These sites identify other users with common interests or backgrounds. Users then decide to include those users as part of their connections or friends.

USED SOCIAL NETWORK SITES

MySpace and Facebook are two of the most notable social networking sites, especially for kids and teens. But there are hundreds of others on the Internet. More than five out of ten teens use social networking sites.

Twitter is another example of a social networking site but it includes a micro-blogging service that lets you send and read other users' updates referred to as tweets. These text posts are displayed on the user's profile page. Like all social networking sites, you must be careful about giving out personal information and not respond to users you don't know.

These sites are really quite amazing and efficient. Signing up requires no real-age verification. There is also no way to verify that information presented on the site is valid. It's all left up to individual users. But once you're on a site, you only need to enter a small amount of information before the system starts identifying potential "friends." Information posted on the site can be public or private. It can include pictures, videos, and text.

 A New York teenager has sued Facebook and some of its users because of a Facebook chat group where she says she was ridiculed and disgraced. (Jones, 2009)

Social networking sites are virtual societies within our real society. And like in all societies, there are good, bad, and outright dangerous people. But you can't have a social network without them. Even site owners and operators who want to keep sites clean can't do it. They may be able to monitor content, but there is no way to determine the intent or values of those using the sites.

As mentioned earlier, the use of social networking sites continues to grow to the point that even employers are using them as part of the interview process. Things a kid posts to a social networking site today could come back to haunt them years later. And remember: things that happen in cyberspace stay in cyberspace—forever.

Virtual Worlds

Virtual worlds combine aspects of social networking sites with a computer-generated world that its users inhabit and interact with other users using avatars. Avatars are graphic characters customized by users to depict their virtual self. Some are simple, like those found in "Club Penguin." Some adult worlds offer three-dimensional characters that are lifelike in "every" way.

If you have a young child, chances are you've heard of Club Penguin, a Disney site. Your avatar is a penguin and everyone lives in igloos. It seems perfectly safe. But remember: there is no real-age verification, so adults can log in as kids. The result is cyber sharks in the kiddy pool.

Predators going through popular sites such as Disney's Club Penguin were stealing children's earned virtual money and threatening to keep it unless the kids sent images of themselves or engaged them in some way. (Miranda, 2008)

The other side of the story is adult avatar sites like Second Life. It's a place where people have fantasy avatars, buy fantasy products, and live fantasy lives of every sort. It also involves sexual fantasy and deviant behavior. Again, there is no age verification. In these cases kids can sign up as adults and can look and act as they like, without any supervision. It can be pretty kinky.

Second Life is potentially one of the most dangerous places on the web for kids and teens to explore their sexuality and dark sides. It's a world where every man is handsome and ripped and all women are thin with large breasts dressed in very little clothing. Using provocative avatar bodies, kids can be as sexy and intimate as they want to be. Worst than that, their partners can be anyone including sexual predators.

Chat Rooms

The good news about social networking sites is that less than a third of unwanted solicitations come through them. Instant messaging (IM) and chat rooms are much more likely to deliver unsolicited sex chat.

PARTICIPATED IN CHAT ROOMS

Chat rooms are extremely popular modes of Internet communication used by kids to start and nurture online relationships. Over 50% of underage Internet users are chat participants. Conversations are typed on a computer and happen in real time. They can be public or private, and you must join a chat room to participate. There are chat rooms on just about every topic imaginable, from football chat to dating and music chat.

In public chat rooms, a number of kids take part in a conversation at the same time. In a private chat room, kids have one-to-one chats, and it is here that they must be the most cautious. Some chat rooms are monitored by either an employee of the company offering the service or a volunteer. Their purpose is to keep conversations clean and under control.

Depending on the chat room, conversations can get fairly explicit. In a public chat room everyone present can see the conversation. Kids can mutually agree to leave the public chat room and have a private chat where the conversation often gets more personal and potentially more explicit. You only need to imagine what might happen next.

Whether it's chatting or texting, kids have their own lingo for talking to one another. This was brought to the forefront recently in TV commercials that featured "My BFF Jill" (Best Friends Forever).

Chat and Texting Lingo

A/S/L?	Age/Sex/Location?	KOTC	Kiss on the cheek
DOM	Dirty old man	KOTL	Kiss on the lips
EG	Evil grin	LUWAMH	Love you with all my heart
F2F	Face to face	NIFOC	Naked in front of computer
FMTYEWTK	Far more than you ever wanted to know	PAW	Parents are watching
FTBOMH	From the bottom of my heart	POS	Parent over shoulder
H&K	Hug and kiss	SUAKM	Shut up and kiss me
ILU (or ILY)	I love you	TOY	Thinking of you
IPN	I'm posting naked	WEG	Wicked evil grin
IWALU	I will always love you	WTGP?	Want to go private?

Kids Do Dumb Things

There is one last topic to consider when talking about cyber sharks. *Even smart kids do dumb things*. That's just the nature of being a kid. Driven by curiosity, peer pressure, or to just try something, kids screw up every now and then. Since technology is a multiplier, even simple mistakes can have a big impact.

And sometimes those dumb things can get their parents into trouble. Dumb things include giving away passwords, posting inappropriate material, or simply experimenting with things to satisfy their youthful curiosity. Many kids, for example, see no problem with sharing music files or downloading pirated software. Dumb? Yes. But is it dangerous or criminal? As was discussed before, the music industry takes it seriously enough to file lawsuits.

Sexting

The best example of dumb but dangerous things kids do online may be *sexting*. Sexting is the practice of taking nude pictures of one's self and texting them to others. Sexting is a more recent practice that has picked up in popularity with teens. Two of ten kids admit to sending nude or semi-nude pictures of themselves to others. Some kids shrug it off as something that everyone does these days. But that's not the way law enforcement sees it. To them it's child pornography.

Whether you agree with the law or not, it is illegal to take and distribute nude pictures of someone under 18 and send them to others. Anyone who does is breaking the law, and anyone convicted of breaking such a law must register as a sex offender. And that's exactly what's happening to kids who are caught sexting.

 Posting nude pictures of underage kids on a social networking site is also illegal. Recently a 14-year old girl in New Jersey was charged with child pornography after posting nude pictures of herself on her MySpace page.(Associated Press (AP), 2009)

The problem goes deeper. Anyone who receives a nude picture can easily and quickly pass it along to others. And like everything else in the cyber world, these pictures never go away. So while some see sexting as harmless fun, it has life-damaging implications under the current laws.

 Three high school girls who sent semi-nude photos, and four male students who received the photos, were hit with child pornography charges. A 15-year-old high school girl faced similar charges for sending her own racy cell phone photos to classmates. (Irvine, 2009)

Jason on Sexting

 We asked Jason if he had ever received any nude pictures, and he had. Turns out a friend of his was "totally pissed" at a girlfriend. He told Jason that she had sent him nude pictures, and he immediately emailed one to Jason.

When we asked Jason if he had told his parents, he said, "Nope, I just deleted it." Then we told him that you really can't totally delete anything from a computer—that it was still there somewhere and could easily be found. His response: "Are you kidding? How do they do that?"

Jason didn't know what he should have done, nor did his dad. Jason should have told his parents. His parents should have contacted the girl's parents and let them know what was going on.

There are tons of potential problems here. The main point is that some girl's nude picture is being passed around the Internet and could show up anytime, anywhere, and for any reason. All the deletes in the world won't make it go away.

Risks and Consequences

Each type of cyber shark comes with its own set of risk. On the low end of the spectrum is exposure to viruses that could infect your computer and create havoc with your hard drive. At the extreme end is sexual assault and death. And there are many risk levels in between. Beyond exposure to adult content, your kids' reputations may be on the line. And if they are lured into illegal activity, they (or rather, you) may get sued.

CyberShark Risk Summary

CyberShark	Viruse	Exposure	Reputation	Law Suit	Addiction	Jail Time	Harm	Death
Adult / XXX	△	△			△			
Gambling					△	△		
Warez/Hacking	△		△	△	△			
Drugs					△	△	△	△
Identity Thieves			△				△	
Bullies			△				△	△
Sexual Predators							△	△
Sexting		△	△	△		△		

CHAPTER 4

The Kid Factor

Understanding how your kid will act and interact online requires knowing their level of curiosity, the extent to which peer pressure impacts their actions, and their willingness to take risks.

 "We must encourage kids to beware of interacting online with people they don't know. We can help prevent kids from becoming victims by teaching them to be cyber-savvy." (The United States Department of Justice, 2009)

Each Kid Is Unique

Understanding what motivates your kids and drives individual activity is really about parenting. Our goal here is not to teach you how to be a good parent, but rather to help you understand parenting your unique kid in the context of the Internet.

Curiosity, peer pressure, and a willingness to take risks are all a natural part of most young lives. The Internet plays to all three. It used to be that we would ask questions and use books or our imagination to satisfy our curiosity. Today, we do a Google search. No question needs to go unanswered, and the answers are detailed and graphic.

Social networking sites and chat groups involve a great deal of peer-to-peer interaction. In chat groups, kids are talking to kids with others present. Social networking sites are like a big public bulletin board that expose individual information and encourage peer-to-peer activity. By design, they count on peer and group interaction to function.

The extent to which one takes risk is directly tied to the consequences. In too many cases, kids don't understand the consequences of inappropriate Internet activity or simply believe there aren't any. So it's not like they are taking any risk at all.

The anonymity offered by the Internet and use of nicknames embolden kids to take more risks than normal. They believe they can say what they want because no one knows who they are.

Graphing a Kid's Unique Factors

There are other things to consider. For example, is your kid *cyber-smart* and *cyber-savvy*? Being cyber-smart is the extent to which they under-stand how to use and leverage the technology. Being cyber-savvy is a lot like being street-smart. How aware are they of how the Internet is being used and of how some people misuse it to manipulate kids' activities?

Another important consideration is the age factor. Too many people offering solutions to the cyber shark problem divide kids into convenient groups, typically by age. For example, kids under 12 can't look at porn. Kids 18 and older can look at adult sites, and so on. It's the movie-rating approach, and it just doesn't work for the Internet. The Internet is much more complex than watching a movie. Age may be a starting point, but it does not address how an individual child may respond to cyber shark attacks.

Curiosity and the Internet

Curiosity may have killed the cat, but it fed the mouse. More than anything, the Internet is a repository of information that is instantly accessible by anyone with access. If a kid has a question, the answer is online. And kids have tons of questions. You only need to remember some of the questions you had as a kid to imagine what's being searched on Google today.

Every search, no matter how innocent, increases the probability that a kid will be exposed to inappropriate material, whether they are looking for it or not. Therefore, the greater the curiosity, the higher the risk of cyber shark attacks.

 A report from Crisp Wireless finds that "the words "sex" and "porno" are among the most popular terms on mobile search engines." (USA Today, 2008)

Peer Pressure

Just as with other aspects of a young person's life, peer pressure is a driving factor in online activity. It is another vital factor in setting up effective rules for online activity.

The interactive side of the Internet is all about peer relationships. You can't have a social networking site without them. Kids are driven either by the need to be accepted into these networks or by the fear of being rejected and even bullied by them. The Internet dramatically magnifies those needs.

The extent to which your kids succumb to peer pressure determines how they might react to, and interact in, social networking situations. That can include anything from what they post on their sites to what they say in a chat group. Participating in cyber-bullying is a case in point. It's easy to be drawn into conversations that bash or harass someone else when everyone is doing it.

The same applies to content. There are some fairly provocative pictures and a lot of questionable content that's posted on social networking sites. Too many times, kids access and post this kind of content simply because everyone else is doing it.

Technology has become as much a status symbol as it has become anything else. For example, it's not enough to have a cell phone; kids must have the *right* phone. It is even a fashion accessory. Likewise, kids need to be on MySpace or Facebook because everyone else in their class is on that site.

No Fear

For the most part, kids are fearless. And the Internet makes it easier for them to experiment and try new things than ever before. No 12-year-old can step into a real-world casino, drop a couple of bucks into a slot machine, and see what it's like to gamble. But they can do it online.

Unsupervised online activity gives a kid access to a world of things that they could have never experienced just a decade ago. Kids interested in drugs of all kinds can get them online. They can chat with strangers, even adults, experiment with sex, or learn how to build a bomb.

 A Microsoft Canada survey of kids ages 9 to 17, conducted by Youthography, says, "Too many children and teens still engage in risky online behavior, such as posting personal information, accessing adult sexual material, and cyber bullying." (Rynor, 2009)

It's not only the vastness of online information or activities available; it's also the relatively private and seemingly secure way they can take place. Kids can gamble or view porn from their bedrooms. And since they don't recognize or believe there is a risk, the willingness to try anything increases.

Understanding your kid's fear factor helps determine their vulnerability to cyber sharks who might lure them to places they don't belong.

Cyber-Smart

Some kids use the Internet and technology, while others learn from and thrive on it. They can do just about anything, from create a web site to hack someone else's web site. It's a skill particularly amazing to parents who themselves are still trying figure out what the Internet is all about.

Knowing the Internet and technology means knowing what's possible, and the answer is "almost anything." The more cyber-smart your kid is, the more susceptible they are to even greater online dangers. They seek out like-minded friends who share ideas, information, and tricks and tips about things that can be done online.

For the most part, this is a good thing. Self-taught computer experts often make the best programmers. And no matter what their future endeavors, knowing the Internet and technology will add value to their careers.

But there is a dark side. Many computer viruses are created by young hackers who are seeking nothing more than fame and notoriety. And there are plenty of sites that show kids how to hack computer games, get stolen credit cards, and more.

The point is this: The more kids know about the Internet, the more exposed they are to its darker side. It is even more critical that cyber-smart kids understand potential risks and that you pay particular attention to their Internet activity and habits.

Cyber-Savvy

Even kids know that surviving on the Internet requires them to be cyber-savvy. It's like being street-smart, only online. The more cyber–savvy they are, the less likely they are to fall victim to a shark attack.

Being cyber-savvy means having a general awareness of the kinds of things that are happening online and within your local cyber community. There are countless stories about consequences of inappropriate surfing or online interaction. We've called out a small sample throughout this book.

It's equally important to understand what's happening online in your community and schools. Who are the local cyber bullies? They are there and online right now. Who's in the local social networking groups such as those for his or her school and graduating class? The more savvy you and your kids are about Internet activity and the consequences, the less your kids risk being attacked by a cyber shark.

Jason's Cyber-savvyness

Jason is a typical curious kid. If he has a question, he goes to the Internet to find the answer. And he also gets sidetracked. As Jason explains, "When I was looking up "animé" on 4chan I noticed the adult section. So I took a look at it. It was no big deal."

He's also very conscious about what his friends think of him, but not overly concerned about it. And he clearly has no fear. Bottom line: Jason goes anywhere online he pleases.

He's pretty cyber-smart and somewhat cyber-savvy. He won't be hacking someone's password, but he has friends who can do it. He has some idea of what's right and wrong but still has lots to learn.

The good news is he's willing to talk about it. But he needs to be asked the right questions. Another adult had asked Jason about online porn this way: "You don't look at porn sites, do you?" His answer: "Ah, no." Our questioning went like this. "We know that four out of ten kids look at adult sites. Which ones do you look at?" His answer: "Well, I just look at a few."

CHAPTER 5

Shark Repellent

The only way to be certain that you won't be attacked by a shark is to stay out of dangerous water.

It's Not About Trust

Whenever we ask parents what they do to protect their kids when they are online, the most common answer is that they trust their kids. While this is an admirable answer, understanding and protecting kids online is not about trust. More often than not, kids don't set out to do bad or wrong things on the Internet. As we emphasized in the previous chapter, they are drawn in by natural curiosity and peer pressure, or have been exposed to information that they weren't looking for in the first place.

It's not your kids you can't trust. It's everyone and everything online trying to interact with them. Your kids may know right from wrong, and you may trust them to do the right thing. But armed only with that, they have very limited ability to fend off cyber shark attacks. It's an unfair advantage, and the bad guys have it.

The answer: *Trust but verify.* Yes, trust your kids. But when it comes to the Internet, verify that they are doing the right things.

Planning Your Defense

Unlike other Internet-related problems such as viruses, spamming, or spyware, there is no single defense that will protect all kids from all cyber sharks. While technology can help prevent many cyber shark attacks, building the right defense for you and your kids involves a multiprong approach.

Protecting your kids requires that you:

- ☐ Understand the Internet and cyber sharks.

- ☐ Talk to your kids about their Internet activity, the risks, and the consequences.

- ☐ Use appropriate technology to help with the problem, like blocking access to bad sites (shark-infested waters).

- ☐ Trust but verify. Monitor your kids' Internet and cell phone activity.

- ☐ Know what's happening in open waters, outside your virtual world.

Remember that the Internet is dynamic and therefore your plan must be dynamic. Technology and trends continually change. So do your kids. You must frequently talk to your kids about their online activity and review and adjust your plan accordingly.

Get and Stay Smart

The information provided in this book goes a long way in helping you understand the Internet and cyber sharks. Keep in mind that understanding the Internet and its dangers is not a destination; it is a never-ending journey. Things change quickly and often in cyberspace. You need to be aware of, and stay current on, Internet trends.

You can address this issue by using reliable online sources that keep you updated on both new technologies and reported threats. Search engines offer alert systems that notify you of stories based on a topic you select. Google Alerts uses email updates to notify you of the latest relevant Google results (web, news, and so on) based on your choice of query or topic. Yahoo! Alerts is a free, personalized notification service that instantly informs you of what you consider important and relevant via email, instant message, pager, or cell phone.

You can find additional help at the CyberPatrol web site (www.cyberpatrol.com). Our learning center gives you up-to-date information on the topics covered in this book and keeps you informed about kids and their cyber activity.

Define Risk and Rules

With little or no exception, experts agree that the best step you can take to protect kids online is to engage in a conversation with them, explain the risks, and set up the rules. The challenge here is getting started. Some experts recommend using a contract between you and your kid to define the rules. The kid-parent contract seems to be the preferred method to negotiate everything from driving privileges to homework.

The most appropriate course of action is to do what you know works best with your kids. Since they probably know more about the Internet than you do, you might start by asking them to explain a few things to you. Ask them what they know about Facebook or MySpace. Set up your own Facebook site and have them help. Don't ask questions that can be answered with a simple yes or no. And let them know that you know what's going on with kids and the Internet.

However you approach your kid, the most important things to communicate are the risks and dangers associated with unsafe Internet surfing and chatting. Those risks, along with examples, are identified throughout this book. In fact, most kids don't realize that they could get sued, go to jail, or even be molested for things they thought were innocent.

Once you have identified the risks, it's time to set up the rules. As stated earlier, because each kid is unique, the rules will vary from child to child.

Jason on the Risks of Online Contact

 When Jason was about 14, he found and bought something on Craigslist. When it came time to ship the item, the seller asked Jason where he lived. Oddly enough, the seller happened to live nearby and offered to meet him at the local mall to deliver the item he had ordered online.

Fortunately, Jason told his dad, who got involved immediately. Jason let the seller know his dad would be joining him to meet the man at the mall. The seller never showed up. Obviously, the seller wanted to deliver a little more than the item Jason had purchased.

Jason said, "I had no idea that this dude might be coming after me. I learned my lesson from that one. It'll never happen again."

Jason's dad didn't get involved because he was aware of cyber sharks and the potential dangers. He got involved because the situation just didn't seem safe.

Lest you think this is an isolated incident, there is the case of a woman who responded to an ad for a baby-sitter on Craigslist. The person placing the ad claimed to be a working mother named Amy. Actually, it was a 20-year-old male who wanted much more than a baby-sitter. Tragically, he murdered the woman who responded to the advertisement. (Murphy, 2009)

In another case, a 23-year-old Canadian man was hired through an Internet classified advertisement. He used the child he was baby sitting to make a pornographic video. (Pheifer, 2008)

Online Rules for Kids

Keep the rules simple, direct, and to the point. If your kids have to refer to a long document just to understand what they can and cannot do, the rules won't work. Consider color-printing, laminating, and posting them next to the computer. Make them look important enough to follow.

As a starting point, think beyond your house. The old adage that restricts computer use to a public place in your home isn't enough. Kids can get Internet access almost anywhere.

Here is a sample list of rules:

- ☐ Don't talk to or chat with cyber strangers.
- ☐ Don't take cyber candy from a stranger.
- ☐ Don't chat with adults.
- ☐ No sexting or posting of sexy pictures.
- ☐ Don't pass along pictures you've received.
- ☐ Don't give away or post personal information to anyone, ever.
- ☐ Parents get all passwords that kids use.
- ☐ No meetings with people you met online.
- ☐ Tell parents of any problems or suspicions.
- ☐ When in doubt, don't do it.

(These rules are reprinted at the end of this book, so that you can remove a copy for use in your household.)

Remember: There must be consequences if the rules are broken. Otherwise, all you have done is create a wish list. Make sure your kids understand and agree to the penalties for breaking the rules.

You should require that your kids provide you with their user names and passwords to all email, social networking, chat, and other accounts. This requirement sends a message that at any time you may go into their accounts and look at what they have posted or find out with whom they are chatting. This is not an easy task. Kids want their privacy. But when they come to you and ask if they can have a Facebook or MySpace account, make giving you their user names and passwords a condition of their having the account.

Technical Solutions

There is a wide range of software packages and services you can use to block bad sites, monitor online activity, and search the Internet for any information written about your kids that others may have put online. All these tools can help you defend your kids against cyber sharks.

Parental Controls Software

Parental controls software has been around for a while, and the latest versions are quite comprehensive. Don't equate this with the parental controls that block access to movies on your TV. It's much more than that. At its core is the ability to filter and block web sites based on their content. It keeps your kids out of shark-infested waters.

Adding parental controls software to your computer is the most cost-effective and reliable thing you can do to keep your kids away from bad web sites and attracter cyber sharks. *There is no reason any kid should go to these types of sites accidentally or on purpose.* And although your kids may never seek out these sites, they will eventually get there by accident, through a link sent from a friend, by a misspelled URL, or by some other innocent means, unless you use parental controls software.

The better packages, like CyberPatrol, are fairly sophisticated and allow you to block sites based on categories that typically include adult, XXX, gambling, drug sites, and more.

Unlike parental controls that may come with security suites or search engine toolbars, dedicated stand-alone versions offer comprehensive and flexible protection. Parental controls software may also include features to control time spent on a computer, monitor chats and other messages, and protect your kids against sending personal information.

A view of the CyberPatrol (v7.7) Option Selection dialog box

CyberPatrol, for example, lets you personalize settings for each kid who uses your computer. You can also create your own "blacklist" to block certain sites you specify, or "white list" to allow sites that would normally be blocked.

Kid Monitoring

Some parental controls software and other types of monitoring software let you monitor online activity in real time. Think of Internet activity as soccer, hockey, or baseball. Odds are you can name every kid on your child's team, as well as their strengths and weaknesses. But how much do you know about each of their cyber friends? One approach is to create a list of friends with whom your kid can chat. A conversation with anyone not on the list sends you an immediate text message or email alert. Other software provides a log that lets you monitor activity through reports. You can review surfing and chatting patterns and take appropriate action.

Cyber Monitoring

As important as it is to know what's happening on your kid's computer, it's equally critical to know what's going on in the cyber community around you. If, for example, your kid's school had a cyber-bullying problem, you'd want to know about it. And if someone was spreading rumors and lies about your kid online, you'd want to know about that too. Internet monitoring services are available that allow you to do just that.

Normally available for a monthly fee, these services scan the Internet based on information you provide about your kid. For example, they can look for anything being said about an individual kid and include information about cyber activity taking place at that kid's school or in the surrounding community.

Cyber Shark Detector

Whenever we ask parents if their kids may be viewing porn or other bad web sites, the most common answer we get is, "Not my kid." And when we ask how they know, the most common answer is, "Because I asked them and they said they weren't."

CyberPatrol's free *Threat Detector* lets you run a program on your kid's PC that tells you how many bad web sites, if any, they have visited. Since we use stringent controls for sites, it's not unusual to get a very small number of hits. If, however, you see a category with a large number of hits, it's a good indication that whoever is using the PC is going places they shouldn't be going.

THREAT Detector

Status

Scan Complete.

Total Web Sites Found   495

SCAN FOR THREATS

Version   1.0.0.23

Scan Results

1	Adult
0	Alcohol and Tobacco
0	Error or Blank
1	Gambling
1	Hacking and Warez
1	Illegal Activities
2	Parked Domains
1	Spam
12	XXX Rated

Note: CyberPatrol Threat Detector will not retain or share any information that is used during the scan.

Click here for more information regarding your results

A sample of results from a CyberPatrol Threat Detector system scan

CyberPatrol offers this program free because we know you must understand your kid's Internet surfing habits before you can address surfing problems. Asking your kid won't necessarily get you the right answer.

For a free copy of this program, visit our web site at **cyberpatrol.com**.

CHAPTER 6

Create Your Emergency Plan

"Parents and children should remember that a computer-sex offender can be any age or sex. The person does not have to fit the caricature of a dirty, unkempt, older man wearing a raincoat to be someone who could harm a child." (The Federal Bureau of Investigation, 2001)

 No matter what precautions you take, there is always the possibility of a cyber shark attack. If it happens, you need to know in advance what actions to take. Unfortunately, most kids and parents are not prepared. But you can become prepared right now by creating your emergency response plan.

Appropriate actions will vary depending on the type of attack. In some cases, kids need only to notify their parents and possibly change their surfing habits. More serious attacks, such as those by sexual predators or cyber bullies, require notifying the parents, schools, and appropriate authorities.

Responding to a Sexual Predator Attack

Because sexual predators are the worst kind of cyber sharks, their attacks require immediate and decisive action. You must protect your kid, and you must do your best to help catch the predator.

When kids are approached by a sexual predator, they don't always tell their parents. But there are telltale signs that can give you clues that your kids may be under attack.

Here are the warning signs the FBI suggests you look for to determine whether your kids may be at risk:

- Your child spends large amounts of time online, especially at night.

- You find pornography on your child's computer.

- Your child receives phone calls from men you don't know or is making calls, sometimes long distance, to numbers you don't recognize.

- Your child receives mail, gifts, or packages from someone you don't know.

- Your child turns the computer monitor off or quickly changes the screen on the monitor when you come into the room.

- Your child becomes withdrawn from the family.

- Your child is using an online account belonging to someone else.

(The Federal Bureau of Investigation, 2001)

If you believe your child may have become a target of a sexual predator, or if you notice some or all of the signs listed here, you must take action.

Talk with your kid openly about your suspicions and find out as much information as you can.

Look at what's on their computer and social networking sites. Track and monitor emails, chat rooms, and text messages. The FBI's "A Parent's Guide to Internet Safety" (see the bibliography at the end of this book) offers specific examples of activities or events that warrant contacting authorities.

If any of the following situations arise in your household, via the Internet or an online service, you should immediately contact your local or state law enforcement agency, the FBI, and the National Center for Missing & Exploited Children:

• Your child or anyone in your household has received child pornography.

• Your child has been sexually solicited by someone who knows that your child is under 18 years of age.

• Your child has received sexually explicit images from someone who knows that your child is under 18 years of age.

According to the FBI, "If one of these scenarios occurs, keep the computer turned off in order to preserve any evidence for future law enforcement use. Unless directed to do so by the law enforcement agency, you should not attempt to copy any of the images and/or text found on the computer." (The Federal Bureau of Investigation, 2001)

Responding to a Cyber-Bully Attack

Cyber-bullying has become a serious problem, and if it happens to your kid, you need to take it seriously. It can have a detrimental psychological and emotional impact on your kid.

Again, your kid may not tell you when this is happening. Remember that kids normally won't talk about these things unless you ask them. Warning signs can include nightmares, absence from school, or a sudden disinterest in their computer or the Internet. It's almost as if they want to run away and hide from the bullying.

Cyber-bullying also requires decisive action. If your kid becomes a victim of a bullying attack, consider the following actions:

- Don't respond to the cyber-bullying online.

- Save any pictures or messages as evidence.

- Try to identify the persons responsible.

- Report the incident to your kid's school.

- If possible, block the cyber bullies from future contact.

- Contact the bullies' parents.

- Report any incident of online harassment and physical threats to your local police and to your Internet service provider (ISP).

Porn, Illegal File Sharing and Other Bad Sites

If you find out that your kid is viewing porn, down-loading or sharing music illegally, gambling, or going to other bad web sites, talk to them about the problem. And as soon as you have done that, buy parental controls software for your computer and block those sites.

CHAPTER 7

Safer Waters

As in the real world, there will always be risks and potential problems with using the Internet. Talking with your kids about their cyber activity and taking a few precautions greatly reduces the probability that they will become victims of a cyber shark attack. The whole idea is to make the waters that they surf in safer.

Our stories from Jason highlight a key point. Cyber shark attacks are not a one-time event that happens to a small group of kids. Cyber dangers are ever present, and kids can become victims simply by being kids. So even if you trust your kids to make good value judgments, they're still vulnerable. As parents, we have a responsibility to protect them the best that we can.

Think about this. Since the creation of the Internet we have all been exposed to viruses, spam, malware, phishing, spyware, and a host of other computer threats. By now we have learned that we must have security software running on our PCs or an attack is inevitable. We can lose our identity, have data destroyed, and even have our PC trashed. So we take action.

Cyber shark attacks can put our PCs at risk, but more importantly, they put our kids at risk. Yet by some accounts, only about three in ten families have parental controls software running on their computers. Many parents rely on free or integrated software that comes as part of a suite, operating system, or search toolbar. Too many of these programs don't offer complete protection, and some focus only on adult content. It's not comprehensive enough.

Using parental controls software is one of the simplest and most effective steps you can take to protect your kids. If nothing else, it blocks access to sites that kids have no business going to in the first place. Moreover, it offers additional tools to monitor or block chat, control computer access, and report on activity.

 "To minimize chances of an on-line exploiter victimizing your child ...utilize parental controls provided by your service provider and/or blocking software." (The Federal Bureau of Investigation, 2001)

More and more we hear news stories about cyber-bullying, sexting, online predators, and problems with social networking sites. These are the stories that make the headlines. To some degree, these kinds of things happen daily online. It's important to be aware of them. While none of us like to dwell on these kinds of stories, parents especially can't afford to ignore the problem.

Kids need help coping with the online challenges they face daily. The digital divide between many parents and kids may make it difficult to get that help from mom and dad. But what a parent does bring to the table is a good set of values and judgment. Deciding how to address cyber problems requires that and some common sense. So engage your kids and get involved in their cyber lives.

Here's one last point. Our experience with Jason was interesting in that he was eager to share with us what he knew about the Internet. There's something about technology that makes people in general want to share what they know. So when you start asking your kids questions, don't be surprised if you get more than you bargained for.

Use technology to help address the problem. Keep aware of what's happening online and how it might impact your kids. Talk to your kids about their online experiences. These steps will go a long way in making the waters safer for them and less scary for you.

Bibliography

- Aleccia, JoNel. 2009. Problem Gambling May Rise as Economy Falls. MSNBC.com, Jan. 30.

  http://www.msnbc.msn.com/id/28921476/

- Associated Press (AP) 2009. Boy Posing as Girl on Facebook Extorts Sex. CBS News.

  http://www.cbsnews.com/stories/2009/02/05/national/main4777194.shtml.

- Brooks, Nicole. 2009. Students at Greater Risk for Problem Gambling. Herald-Times, March 28. Bloomington, Indiana.

- Childnet.com. Young People, Music & the Internet.

  http://www.childnet-int.org/music/index.html

- Daily Mail Reporter. 2009. Teens Spend Average of 87 Hours a Year Looking at Porn Online. Mail Online. (February 9)

  http://www.dailymail.co.uk/sciencetech/article-1139811/Teens-spend-average-87-hours-year-looking-porn-online.html. UK.

- Federal Bureau of Investigation. *A Parents Guide to Internet Safety*.

  http://www.fbi.gov/publications/pguide/parentsguide.pdf

- Foxnews.com. 2009. Japanese Teen Arrested on Suspicion of Making Bombs to Blow Up Classmates.

  http://www.foxnews.com/story/0,2933,500691,00.html. February 26.

- Gross, Grant. IDG News Service 2009. Supreme Court refuses Internet age restrictions case. January 22.

  http://news.cnet.com/8301-10789_3-10105303-57.html

- Irvine, Martha. 2009. Teens Who Text Racy Photos Charged with Porn. Chicago Tribune, February 14. Chicago, Illinois.

- Jones, K.C.,2009. Facebook Named in Cyber-Bullying Suit. Information Week (March 4).

  http://www.informationweek.com/news/internet/social_network/showArticle.jhtml?articleID=215800519

- Lenhart, Amanda. June 30, 2008. Teens, Online Stranger Contact & Cyberbullying: What the research is telling us.

  http://www.pewinternet.org/Presentations/2008/Teens-Online-Stranger-Contact--Cyberbullying.aspx   Pew Internet & American Life Project. Washington, DC.

- Maher, Damian. 2008. Cyberbullying: An ethnographic case study of one Australian upper primary school class. Youth Studies Australia vol. 27, no. 4, 50-57.

- McAfee. 2008. Teen/Mom Internet Survey.

  http://us.mcafee.com/en-us/local/docs/Moms'%20fears%20and%20teen%20behavior%20online.pdf

- Miranda, Charles. 2008. Child sex predators use blackmail tactic over internet. Courier Mail of Australia, November 01.

- Murphy, Esme. 2009. Defense: Death Was Accidental in Craigslist Murder. WCOO.com, March 23.

  http://wcco.com/crime/craigslist.murder.trial.2.966051.html

- Neuburger, Jeffrey D. 2009. U.S. Supreme Court (Finally) Kills Online Age Verification Law. PBS.org, January 29.

  http://www.pbs.org/mediashift/2009/01/us-supreme-court-finally-kills-online-age-verification-law029.html

- Palfrey, John, Dena Sacco, Danah Boyd, Laura DeBonis, and Internet Safety Technical Task Force. 2009. Enhancing Child Safety and Online Technologies: Final Report of the Internet Safety Technical Task Force to the Multi-State Working Group on Social Networking of State Attorneys General of the United States. Berkman Center for Internet & Society: Harvard University. Cambridge, MA.

- Pheifer, Pat. 2008. Craigslist baby sitter pleads guilty to child pornography. Star Tribune, December 4. Minneapolis, MN

- Rynor, Becky. 2009. Canadian Kids Taking Risks Online: Survey. Montreal Gazette, February 26.
  http://www.montrealgazette.com/Technology/Canadian+kids+taking+risks+online+survey/1329813/story.html

- Schonfeld, Erick.,2009. Thousands Of MySpace Sex Offender Refugees Found On Facebook. TechCrunch.com (February 3)
  http://www.techcrunch.com/2009/02/03/thousands-of-myspace-sex-offender-refugees-found-on-facebook/

- Swedlund, Eric. 2008. Music industry sues 14 at UA; file shares alleged. Arizona Daily Star, February 29. Tucson, AZ.

- The National Campaign to Prevent Teen and Unplanned Pregnancy. Sex and Tech: Results from a Survey of Teens and Young Adults.
  http://www.thenationalcampaign.org/sextech/PDF/SexTech_Summary.pdf.

- The National Center for Missing and Exploited Children. 2009 Online Victimization of Youth: 5 Years Later.
  http://www.missingkids.com/en_US/publications/NC167.pdf

- The Partnership for a Drug-Free America. 2009. The Partnership Attitude Tracking Study (PATS) Teen 2008 Report.
  http://www.drugfree.org/Files/full_report_teens_2008

- The United States Department of Justice. 2009. Helping Create Cyber-Savvy Kids.

  http://www.justice.gov/usao/ut/psc/documents/ESD_CyberSafety.pdf

- The Wired Campus. 2008, December 4. "MySpace Profile Can Cost Student-Teacher Her Degree, Judge Says."

  http://chronicle.com/wiredcampus/article/3503/online-drunken-pirate-photo-can-cost-student-her-degree-judge-says

- USA Today, 2009. USA Today.com. (June 13)

  http://www.usatoday.com/money/advertising/adtrack/2008-06-08-adtrack-mrbill_N.htm.

- Vamosi, Robert. 2008. How to Handle ID Fraud's Youngest Victims. CNET News, November 21.

- Web of Trust (WOT). 2008, June. "WOT Finds Increased Security Threats in the Internet's Red Light District: Adult Sites Cause the Most Damage to Internet Users."

  http://www.mywot.com/en/press/wot-study-internets-red-light-district

Online Rules for Kids

Here is the same sample list of rules for kids using the Internet, printed previously from page 85. We've reprinted it here so that you can cut it out and use it in your own home.

Internet Rules

- ☐ Don't talk to or chat with cyber strangers.
- ☐ Don't take cyber candy from a stranger.
- ☐ Don't chat with adults.
- ☐ No sexting or posting of sexy pictures.
- ☐ Don't pass along pictures you've received.
- ☐ Don't give away or post personal information to anyone, ever.
- ☐ Parents get all passwords that kids use.
- ☐ No meetings with people you met online.
- ☐ Tell parents of any problems or suspicions.
- ☐ When in doubt, don't do it.

::: Surfing With The Cyber Sharks